ENDANGERED AND THREATENED ANIMALS

THE WALLABY

A MyReportLinks.com Book

Kim A. O'Connell

MyReportLinks.com Books
an imprint of
Enslow Publishers, Inc.
Box 398, 40 Industrial Road
Berkeley Heights, NJ 07922
USA

MyReportLinks.com Books, an imprint of Enslow Publishers, Inc. MyReportLinks®
is a registered trademark of Enslow Publishers, Inc.

Library of Congress Cataloging-in-Publication Data

O'Connell, Kim A.
  The wallaby / Kim A. O'Connell.
    p. cm. — (Endangered and threatened animals)
  Includes bibliographical references (p.).
  ISBN 0-7660-5064-5
  1. Wallabies—Juvenile literature. 2. Endangered species—Juvenile literature. I. Title. II. Series.
  QL737.M35O29 2005
  599.2'2—dc22

                                2004009698

Printed in the United States of America

10 9 8 7 6 5 4 3 2 1

To Our Readers:
Through the purchase of this book, you and your library gain access to the Report Links that
specifically back up this book.
The Publisher will provide access to the Report Links that back up this book and will keep these Report
Links up to date on **www.myreportlinks.com** for five years from the book's first publication date.
We have done our best to make sure all Internet addresses in this book were active and appropriate
when we went to press. However, the author and the Publisher have no control over, and assume
no liability for, the material available on those Internet sites or on other Web sites they may link to.
The usage of the MyReportLinks.com Books Web site is subject to the terms and conditions stated
on the Usage Policy Statement on **www.myreportlinks.com**.
A password may be required to access the Report Links that back up this book. The password is
found on the bottom of page 4 of this book.
Any comments or suggestions can be sent by e-mail to comments@myreportlinks.com or to the
address on the back cover.

Photo Credits: © Australian Native Wildlife Gallery, p. 26; © Corel Corporation, pp. 1, 3,
15, 19, 25, 29, 30, 31, 32, 38, 44; © Macquarie University, p. 39; © Painet Stock Photos,
p. 42; Animal Info, p. 21; Arkive.org, p. 35; Clipart.com, p. 10; Department for
Environment and Heritage, Government of South Australia, p. 37; Enslow Publishers,
Inc., p. 12; Jiri Lochman/Lochman Transparencies, p. 24; John Bavaro, p. 17; Lamington
National Park, p. 20; Museum Victoria, pp. 11, 22; MyReportLinks.com Books, p. 4;
Unisense Foundation, p. 41.

Cover Photo: Kakadu Park wallaby, © Corel Corporation.

Contents

MyReportLinks.com Books
Great Books, Great Links, Great for Research!

The Internet sites listed on the next four pages can save you hours of research time. These Internet sites—we call them "Report Links"—are constantly changing, but we keep them up to date on our Web site.

Give it a try! Type http://www.myreportlinks.com into your browser, click on the series title, then the book title, and scroll down to the Report Links listed for this book.

The Report Links will bring you to great source documents, photographs, and illustrations. MyReportLinks.com Books save you time, feature Report Links that are kept up to date, and make report writing easier than ever!

Please see "To Our Readers" on the copyright page for important information about this book, the MyReportLinks.com Web site, and the Report Links that back up this book.

Please enter **EWA1781** if asked for a password.

Report Links

The Internet sites described below can be accessed at
http://www.myreportlinks.com

*EDITOR'S CHOICE

▶ Animal Info—Banded Hare Wallaby

The banded hare wallaby probably became extinct on the Australian mainland by 1963 but still exists on several islands. Learn about this wallaby species at this site.

Link to this Internet site from http://www.myreportlinks.com

*EDITOR'S CHOICE

▶ Yellow-footed Rock Wallaby

Yellow-footed rock wallabies were once common in Australia, but early colonists shot them for sport. Presently, they are ravaged by feral goats and foxes. At this site, learn how many are left and what people are doing to save them.

Link to this Internet site from http://www.myreportlinks.com

*EDITOR'S CHOICE

▶ Rufous Hare Wallaby *(Lagorchestes hirsutus)*

This Web site includes information on the rufous hare wallaby, also known as the western hare wallaby, mala, and spinifex rat.

Link to this Internet site from http://www.myreportlinks.com

*EDITOR'S CHOICE

▶ Bridled Nail-tailed Wallaby, *Onychogalea fraenata*

Loss of ground cover has left the bridled nail-tailed wallaby more vulnerable to attacks from feral cats and foxes. At this site, see why sheep, cattle, and rabbits, combined with droughts and land development, have taken their toll on this species.

Link to this Internet site from http://www.myreportlinks.com

*EDITOR'S CHOICE

▶ Dreaming Online: An Introduction to Indigenous Australia

This Australian Museum site offers a comprehensive look at Australia's Aboriginal people, who have had both a positive and negative effect on the country's wallaby population.

Link to this Internet site from http://www.myreportlinks.com

*EDITOR'S CHOICE

▶ Whiptail Wallaby: Mammals of Lamington National Park

A wallaby species found in Lamington National Park in Queensland, Australia, is the whiptail wallaby, also known as the pretty-face wallaby. This park site includes a brief description of the whiptail.

Link to this Internet site from http://www.myreportlinks.com

 The Internet sites described below can be accessed at
http://www.myreportlinks.com

▶**Animal Info—Bridled Nail-tailed Wallaby**
At this site, learn why the bridled nail-tailed wallaby is an endangered animal.
Loss of habitat and food supply, along with its fur value, are some of the
reasons for its decline.

Link to this Internet site from http://www.myreportlinks.com

▶**Australian Native Wildlife Gallery**
On this Web site you can view photographs and drawings of Australian
wildlife, including those of a few species of extinct wallaby.

Link to this Internet site from http://www.myreportlinks.com

▶**Australian Walkabout: Animals: Parma Wallaby**
The parma wallaby, found only in New South Wales and on Kawau Island,
New Zealand, is a small wallaby with a white moustache marking. Learn more
about this species at this zoo site.

Link to this Internet site from http://www.myreportlinks.com

▶**Bennett's Wallaby *(Macropus rufogriseus rufogriseus)***
This site provides a brief overview of Bennett's wallaby. Information on
the species' habitat, diet, breeding, and more is included.

Link to this Internet site from http://www.myreportlinks.com

▶**Brush-tailed Rock Wallaby—Endangered Species Listing**
The brush-tailed rock wallaby is in decline. This site examines the factors
that are primarily responsible for its near extinction: hunting, predation,
and competition for food.

Link to this Internet site from http://www.myreportlinks.com

▶**Brush-tailed Rock Wallaby Colony Near Goulburn
Given Another Chance for Survival**
At this Australian National Parks site, read about wildlife officials working
with a colony of brush-tailed rock wallabies to save them from extinction.
Links to information about other wallaby species are included.

Link to this Internet site from http://www.myreportlinks.com

Any comments? Contact us: **comments@myreportlinks.com**

Report Links

→ The Internet sites described below can be accessed at
http://www.myreportlinks.com

▶ **Earth Sanctuaries: Tammar Wallaby**
One of the smallest wallabies in the "big kangaroo" genus, the tammar
wallaby is no longer found on the Australian mainland. At this site,
learn about the tammar and follow links to the Warrawong Earth
Sanctuary, where it is protected.

Link to this Internet site from http://www.myreportlinks.com

▶ **Ecological Use of Fire on Fraser Island**
This site from FIDO, the Fraser Island Defenders Organization,
proposes a fire-management regime based on Aboriginal practices
to increase biodiversity on the Australian island.

Link to this Internet site from http://www.myreportlinks.com

▶ **Endangered Wallabies Benefit From Feral Goat
Control in State's Northwest**
At this site, read about the removal of more than 500 feral goats and pigs
in the area around Mount Kaputar and Warrumbungle National Parks.

Link to this Internet site from http://www.myreportlinks.com

▶ **Family Macropodidae**
Wallabies and kangaroos are marsupials that belong to the Macropod
family. These animals with pouches have powerful hind limbs, with the
fourth toe of the hind foot being the longest and strongest. Learn more
about them at this site.

Link to this Internet site from http://www.myreportlinks.com

▶ **Flinders Ranges National Park**
Australia's Flinders Ranges National Park is home to yellow-footed
rock wallabies, who were nearly driven to extinction by predators,
introduced species, and hunters. The park's Web site also includes
photos and details of other species in the park.

Link to this Internet site from http://www.myreportlinks.com

▶ **Invasive Species: A Case Study of Australia**
European settlers in Australia brought a variety of animals with them,
including foxes, dogs, cats, and birds. At this site, see how introduced
species affect native species, such as wallabies.

Link to this Internet site from http://www.myreportlinks.com

 The Internet sites described below can be accessed at
http://www.myreportlinks.com

▶ The IUCN Red List of Threatened Species

The IUCN–World Conservation Union provides a searchable database of endangered and threatened animal and plant species. It also lists the five most critically endangered animal species in the world today.

Link to this Internet site from http://www.myreportlinks.com

▶ Kangaroos & Wallabies

Learn more about the illegal killing of kangaroos and wallabies in Australia. Some of these animals are trapped, shot, or poisoned and left to suffer.

Link to this Internet site from http://www.myreportlinks.com

▶ Kangaroos and Wallabies: Discovery.com

The red kangaroo and swamp wallaby are common in Australia. The Australia Zoo has one of the largest enclosures anywhere in the world for these marsupials. Read more about these animals that are not endangered.

Link to this Internet site from http://www.myreportlinks.com

▶ Kangaroos and Wallabies: National Parks

The predators of kangaroos and wallabies include people, dingoes, foxes, feral cats, and goats. At this site, learn about these and other factors that affect wallabies' survival.

Link to this Internet site from http://www.myreportlinks.com

▶ Kawau Island Wallabies

Wallabies introduced on the island of Kawau, New Zealand, in the 1870s have caused problems for a variety of native plants and animals. At this site, find out more about the effects of introduced species on entire ecosystems.

Link to this Internet site from http://www.myreportlinks.com

▶ Living With Kangaroos and Wallabies

The Tasmanian pademelon and Bennett's wallaby are two marsupial species living in Tasmania. The forester kangaroo also lives on this island. At this site, read about the problems that these animals can cause landowners.

Link to this Internet site from http://www.myreportlinks.com

Report Links

The Internet sites described below can be accessed at
http://www.myreportlinks.com

▶ Red-Necked Wallaby
This zoo site examines the differences between kangaroos and wallabies.
Though both are marsupials, animals with pouches, wallabies are
smaller and slower than kangaroos.

Link to this Internet site from http://www.myreportlinks.com

▶ Rock Wallabies
This site offers an overview of rock wallabies, small and quick
marsupials that live in areas of rocky hills, cliffs, and gorges.

Link to this Internet site from http://www.myreportlinks.com

▶ Scotia Sanctuary
Scotia is an Australian Wildlife Conservancy sanctuary that helps
threatened species such as bilbies, numbats, and the endangered
bridled nail-tailed wallaby. At Scotia's site, learn about these species.

Link to this Internet site from http://www.myreportlinks.com

▶ Seventy-Seven-Year Mystery Solved Over the Color Purple
A purple mammal of any kind is a rarity, but a purple wallaby?
Read about the efforts of a Macquarie University biologist who has
confirmed that the purple-neck rock wallaby is a distinct species.

Link to this Internet site from http://www.myreportlinks.com

▶ Tammar Wallaby Reintroduction to the South Australian Mainland
At this site, read about one foundation's attempt to reintroduce the
tammar wallaby to the Australian mainland.

Link to this Internet site from http://www.myreportlinks.com

▶ Wallaby Factfile
The similarities and differences between the parma and red-necked
wallabies are examined in this site.

Link to this Internet site from http://www.myreportlinks.com

Scientific Name

In the larger Macropodidae family, most wallabies, including the parma wallaby, belong to the *Macropus* genus. The banded hare wallaby belongs to the genus *Lagostrophus;* the western hare wallaby, *Lagorchestes;* the nail-tails, *Onychogalea;* and the rock wallabies, *Petrogale.*

Habitat/Range

Historically, wallabies have been found throughout mainland Australia, with some populations on smaller off-shore islands and the large island state of Tasmania. Wallabies are also found in New Guinea. Feral wallaby populations can be found in other parts of the world. Traditional habitats range from deserts and woodlands to rocky hills and rain forest.

Average Weight

Smaller wallabies might weigh between 3 and 7 pounds (such as hare wallabies), but larger species, such as swamp wallabies, might weigh 44 pounds or more.

Average Length

From head to base of tail, the average length of wallabies ranges from about 2 to 3 feet (hare wallabies and scrub wallabies) to between 4 and 5 feet (rock wallabies and nail-tailed wallabies).

Life Span

Between 10 and 20 years for most species

Status

Six wallabies are classified as endangered by the United States Fish and Wildlife Service—the banded hare wallaby, western hare wallaby, bridled nail-tailed wallaby, crescent nail-tailed wallaby, yellow-footed rock wallaby, and parma wallaby. It is generally believed that the crescent nail-tailed wallaby, last seen in the 1960s, is extinct.

Coat or Fur Color

Generally reddish, gray, brown, or sandy colored, with various facial or body markings depending on the species

Breeding Season

Breeding can occur at various points throughout the year, although the tammar wallaby has a very defined breeding season.

Gestation Period

Between 3 and 5 weeks, depending on the species

Threats

Predators, habitat loss, competition for food, hunting, and fire

Lost and Found: Rediscovering Wallabies

When an animal becomes extinct, it will never be seen again on Earth. This is why scientists and wildlife activists work so hard to protect animals that are threatened or endangered. Sometimes, however, scientists get lucky. In 1991, the brush-tailed rock wallaby was thought to be extinct in Australia's Warrumbungle National Park. However, in 1993, park staff found fresh wallaby droppings.

Museum Victoria [ed-online] Bioinformatics - Victorian Mammal Database - Microsoft Internet Explorer

File　Edit　View　Favorites　Tools　Help

Address ⏺ http://www.museum.vic.gov.au/bioinformatics/mammals/images/pecllive.htm ▼ ⌀ Go　Links

Done　　　　　　　　　　　　　　　　　🌏 Internet

▲ *The brush-tailed rock wallaby. The name* wallaby *comes from an Australian Aboriginal word,* wolaba.

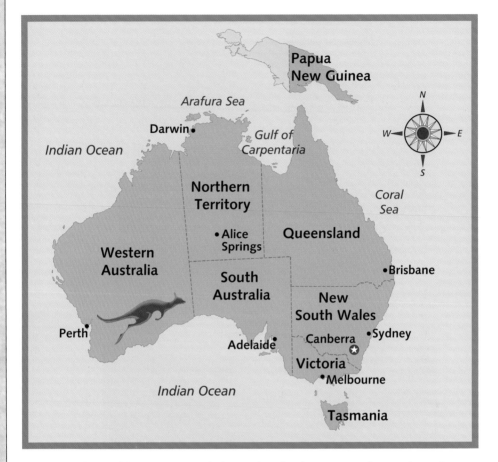

Papua
New Guinea

Arafura Sea

Darwin•

Gulf of
Carpentaria

Indian Ocean

N
W —◉— E
S

Northern
Territory

Coral
Sea

•Alice
Springs

Queensland

Western
Australia

•Brisbane

South
Australia

New
South Wales

Perth•

•Sydney

Adelaide•

Canberra

Victoria

•Melbourne

Indian Ocean

Tasmania

▲ Wallabies are native only to the island-continent of Australia and
Papua New Guinea, part of an island to Australia's north.

Soon afterward, researchers discovered seven small colonies
of rock wallabies in various locations around the park. With
an unexpected opportunity to protect this fragile species,
Australian officials developed a plan to increase the rock
wallaby population.

Found in Australia and Papua New Guinea, wallabies
are some of the world's most endangered species. Like kangaroos, wallabies are marsupials—mammals that lack a

true placenta (the organ that unites a fetus to its mother's uterus). Most marsupials also care for and carry their young in a pouch attached to the abdomen of the mother. Nearly all of Australia's marsupials have suffered from hunting, loss of habitat, and other threats. But introduced species—animals that were brought to Australia from other places—have caused the most damage by preying on native species and competing for food and shelter. In the last two centuries, ten species of Australian marsupials have gone extinct, including some wallabies. "Unless more action is taken now," a researcher from the World Wide Fund for Nature (now known as the WWF) said in 1995, "we will definitely lose more species."[1]

► Rock Wallabies

Brush-tailed rock wallabies look like small kangaroos. But they are distinctive because of their prominent brushy tail, pale stripes on their cheeks, and dark brown or black paws. These wallabies like to shelter in caves or dense clumps of vegetation, and adult males will aggressively defend their claimed area. Despite this, brush-tailed rock wallabies are at risk. Foxes and feral cats and dogs prey on the wallabies and their young. Feral animals are domestic animals that have become wild. Other animals, such as goats, compete with the wallabies for their food. These wallabies are also prone to catching diseases carried by cats or sheep. In the past, the wallabies were hunted for their fur, and some were even shot when they wandered onto nearby farms. In Australia's dry landscape, fire also poses a serious threat to wallaby populations. In 2003, severe wildfires wiped out the entire population of rock wallabies at a nature reserve.

Today, however, the Warrumbungle rock wallabies are making a slow, steady comeback. Park officials are

working to reduce the nearby populations of foxes and goats. Fire management, which includes the setting of controlled beneficial fires to reduce the spread of wildfires, protects wallaby habitat, which also benefits other native species such as possums and koalas. Tourists visiting the national park play an important role too, by treading lightly to limit the disturbance of wallaby colonies. In fact, the park has worked to establish the brush-tailed rock wallaby as a local mascot.

Like the Warrumbungle rock wallaby, several other species of wallabies have been "lost and found" over the years. The parma wallaby, which has a distinctive white throat, had been considered extinct since the 1930s, until an introduced colony was found on a small island off of New Zealand and soon afterward rediscovered in its native Australia. The bridled nail-tailed wallaby was also thought to be extinct until it was found near the town of Dingo, Australia, in the mid-1970s. In 1977, reports of a "tree kangaroo" that was seen near the coast of Queensland, a northeastern state in Australia, led to the discovery of a new species, the Proserpine rock wallaby. These discoveries have allowed researchers to establish recovery programs for these wallabies, offering hope for their survival.

The Real "Big Foot"

The landscape of Australia looks like no other landscape in the world. An Austrian geologist named Eduard Suess came up with a theory, now supported by other geologists, that Australia was once part of a vast supercontinent. He called it Gondwanaland, and it included what are now Antarctica, India, Africa, and South America. Suess's theory said that about 130 million years ago, forces deep under the earth's surface began to slowly break apart Gondwanaland. Eventually, Australia split off as a massive island, carrying many species of animals and plants with it.

▲ Ayers Rock, in Australia's Northern Territory, is the world's largest monolith, or single stone formation. Rock wallabies bound from rocky outcroppings near this often-visited site in the Australian outback.

To survive, Australian plants and animals have adapted special features that are well suited to the often harsh climate and landscape. Chief among these special animals are marsupials, a class of mammals that carry their young in an outside pouch instead of an inside womb. Separated from other landforms, Australia's marsupials evolved into a wide range of species that, with only a few exceptions, are found nowhere else on Earth. These include kangaroos, wallabies, koalas, bandicoots, pademelons, and possums.

Wallabies are basically just small kangaroos. Both belong to a group of marsupials called macropods. These animals have strong hind legs, thick muscular tails, and long feet. In fact, the word *macropod* means "big foot." These animals have relatively short arms and small heads, but their ears are fairly large. Wallabies and kangaroos move by leaps and bounds—jumping quickly from place to place. Their quickness is impressive—they can reach speeds of 31 miles per hour (50 kilometers per hour). More than two dozen species of wallabies are found on the Australian mainland, with some populations on smaller offshore islands and the large island state of Tasmania. Wallabies are also found in Papua New Guinea.

▷ Room to Roam

Wallabies are adapted to a wide range of habitats, from deserts and woodlands to rocky hills and rain forests. Different species are associated with different habitats. The black-striped wallaby typically prefers forested areas with a low level of shrubbery and other vegetation. Banded hare wallabies like to stay in thorny thickets on the edges of swamps. The yellow-footed rock wallaby, as its name suggests, prefers rocky cliffs or ridges. Sometimes, rock wallabies can be found in areas where the landscape is flat, with rocky

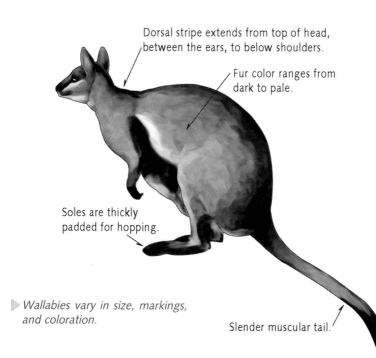

Dorsal stripe extends from top of head, between the ears, to below shoulders.

Fur color ranges from dark to pale.

Soles are thickly padded for hopping.

▷ *Wallabies vary in size, markings, and coloration.*

Slender muscular tail.

outcrops that stick up out of the ground. These outcrops provide shelter for the wallabies.

A few populations of wallabies can be found in areas far away from Australia. For example, an introduced wild population of Bennett's wallabies has thrived in England. The wallabies were brought to England for a private zoo and released during World War II. Similarly, a private zookeeper brought two brush-tailed rock wallabies to Oahu, Hawaii, in 1916. The pair escaped and began to breed. Today, about one hundred rock wallabies are Hawaiian residents.

▷ Birth and Feeding

Marsupials, including wallabies, have short pregnancies that last between three and five weeks. Once the wallabies give birth, their young are only partially developed. Only female marsupials have pouches, which contain four teats. When a

baby wallaby is born, the infant wriggles up to the pouch, where it attaches to one of its mother's teats and feeds on her milk. Called joeys, young kangaroos and wallabies can stay in the pouch for more than two hundred days. Later, when the joey is too big to fit in the pouch, it still drinks its mother's milk from outside her pouch until weaned. The mother will produce different kinds of milk for joeys depending on their age: Joeys still in the pouch receive milk that is high in fats and sugars, while those outside the pouch but still nursing receive a milk high in protein.

As wallabies get older, they begin to graze on many types of plants. Grasses and herbs are the most common food sources for wallabies, but some species also eat leaves, shrubs, and bark. Kangaroos and wallabies have a special digestive system that allows them to absorb nutrients over a longer period of time than other large mammals. In dry seasons, some wallabies can go for long periods without water by chewing on the bark and roots of trees, which retain water. They will also pant, sweat, and lick their arms to stay cool on warm days. Many wallabies are nocturnal, which means that they sleep during the day, seeking cover from the hot sun. Some species might eat in the early morning or late afternoon as well.

▶ Social Creatures

Like kangaroos, wallabies like to feed in groups, which helps to protect them when they eat. When a predator comes across a group of wallabies grazing on the open plains, they will scatter in bounding leaps. "[T]he greater togetherness promoted by grazing became an advantage," writes author John Vandenbeld, "with more eyes to detect danger."[1]

The strongest social relationship of most wallabies is between mothers and their young in-pouch or at-heel

▲ *A wallaby in Kakadu National Park, in Australia's Northern Territory. Agile and rock wallabies are native to Australia's largest national park, which features rock formations that date back 2 million years.*

offspring. As many mammals do, wallabies also smell each other for identification. Joeys also love to play. Often, a joey plays by hopping away from its mother and then returning, then hopping away again and returning. The joey will change direction a lot, as if to keep its mother guessing about where it will go next. Most young males leave the mob, or herd, to become independent as soon as they are old enough. When fights do break out, they are usually between two males competing for a dominant position in the group. These conflicts often resemble boxing or

Back   Forward   Stop   Review   Home   Explore   Favorites   History

http://lamington.nrsm.uq.edu.au/images/fauna/prettyface.JPG - Microsoft Internet Explorer

File   Edit   View   Favorites   Tools   Help

Address   http://lamington.nrsm.uq.edu.au/images/fauna/prettyface.JPG   Go   Links

Done   Internet

▲ Whiptail wallabies in Lamington National Park, Queensland. This
eastern Australian species is also known as the pretty-face wallaby
and is one of the most social species, living in groups of fifty.

wrestling matches, with the addition of karate kicks from the hind legs.

Whiptail wallabies are among the most social of all marsupials. They have been observed in mobs with up to fifty individuals. In a study of whiptail wallabies in New South Wales, Australia, three mobs were found to have slightly overlapping territories. When the mobs crossed paths, wallabies of one group mingled with other groups fairly easily, although grown-up males still fought with each other.

Tools   Search   Notes   Discuss   Go!

Endangered Wallabies

Generally, Australia's largest marsupials, such as red kangaroos and gray kangaroos, are found in large numbers throughout the continent. The smaller marsupials, including wallabies, are at the greatest risk, especially those that belong to the "Critical Weight Range" species, or those species that weigh between 1.2 ounces and 11 pounds (35 grams and 5 kilograms). In the 1990s, the World Conservation Union found that 61 of Australia's 142 marsupial species were threatened with extinction.

The United States Fish and Wildlife Service lists six wallaby species as endangered. These species illustrate the wide

http://www.australianwildlife.org/extinction/images/banded_wallaby_large.jpg - Microsoft Internet Explorer

File   Edit   View   Favorites   Tools   Help

Address http://www.australianwildlife.org/extinction/images/banded_wallaby_large.jpg   Go   Links

Done   Internet

The banded hare wallaby, once found throughout Australia's semiarid regions, is now Western Australia's most threatened marsupial.

▲ *A shy and usually solitary wallaby, the bridled nail-tailed has a pointed "nail" at the end of its tail, which gives it its name. It is also nicknamed "Flash Jack" for its speedy hop.*

differences among wallabies, including their appearances, habitats, and feeding habits. One thing these creatures have in common, however, is that they are all in danger of disappearing if recovery programs are not put into place for all species and such programs are not effective.

Banded Hare Wallaby. Hare wallabies are so named because their small size and behavior reminded their discoverers of hares. Five species of hare wallabies have been identified, although the eastern hare wallaby is considered extinct. The banded hare wallaby is one of the most distinctive hare wallabies, covered in dark bands or stripes that contrast with its gray color. Its fur is thick and soft, and its underbelly is white.

Banded hare wallabies once covered much of Western Australia, where they stayed in thickets near swamps. But Australia's Aboriginal people, the country's first inhabitants, burned the thickets to make hunting easier, and many wallabies were killed in the process. Today, banded hare wallabies are mostly found on islands in Shark Bay. Recently, the Australian Wildlife Conservancy worked to remove feral cats from Faure Island in the hope that banded hare wallabies may one day be relocated there.

Western Hare Wallaby. Also known as the rufous hare wallaby or mala, this species was once found throughout the deserts in the western half of Australia. The western hare wallaby prefers sandy areas that are covered with grass, which forms its primary diet. Fire actually plays a positive role in the western hare wallaby's survival. This species prefers unburned areas for shelter, but it likes to feed on the new grass and brush that grow back after a recent fire.

Bridled Nail-Tailed Wallaby. Nail-tailed wallabies are named for the spur that sticks out of the fur on their tails. They are also known for the distinctive way in which they run, holding their short arms out at a funny angle. Because of this motion, nail-tailed wallabies are sometimes called "organ grinders." The bridled nail-tailed wallaby was once found over most of eastern Australia. The species was considered extinct by the 1930s until a small population was discovered in the 1970s. This animal is notable for the white shoulder stripes that run from its ears, around its shoulders, and onto its underbelly.

Crescent Nail-Tailed Wallaby. The crescent nail-tailed wallaby is similar to the bridled wallaby. The crescent is

smaller and has moon-shaped white markings behind its forearms. Once common in the central and western parts of Australia, the crescent nail-tailed wallaby has not been seen in more than forty years. The species is now thought to be extinct.

Yellow-Footed Rock Wallaby. One of the most colorful wallaby species is the yellow-footed rock wallaby. This species is mostly gray, with a white underbelly. The yellow-footed rock wallaby has a distinct white cheek band and a dark brown stripe that runs from the top of its head down the center of its back. Its ears, forearms, hind legs, and feet can range from a deep orange to a bright yellow. The yellow-footed rock wallaby was once found throughout the isolated desert areas of Australia known as the outback. Now, the species is

▲ *The tiny parma wallaby, whose tail is as long as the rest of its body, is the most critically endangered wallaby species.*

▲ *The island country of New Zealand is home to four wallaby species.*

limited to rocky areas in semidry parts of the states of South Australia and New South Wales, and a subspecies is found in Queensland. The only endangered populations of this species are found in New South Wales. Rock wallaby joeys are threatened by wedge-tailed eagles, foxes, and feral cats. But reintroductions of the species in both Queensland and South Australia have been very successful.

Parma Wallaby. Although still listed as endangered, the white-throated parma wallaby is a potential success story. The small creature was thought to be extinct, suffering from habitat loss and being preyed upon by introduced foxes. In the mid-1960s, a team of scientists discovered several hundred parma wallabies on Kawau Island, New Zealand, and soon afterward the species was found in its native Australia. Foxes remain a threat to this species.

Chapter 3 ▶

Hunting, Habitat Loss, and Other Threats

Off the coast of Queensland, Australia, nearly two dozen colonies of the Proserpine rock wallaby are struggling to survive. First documented in 1976, this shy animal has the smallest known distribution of any of the rock wallabies. In 1997, two of the Queensland wallaby colonies could be found on Mandalay Point, a scenic and popular resort area.

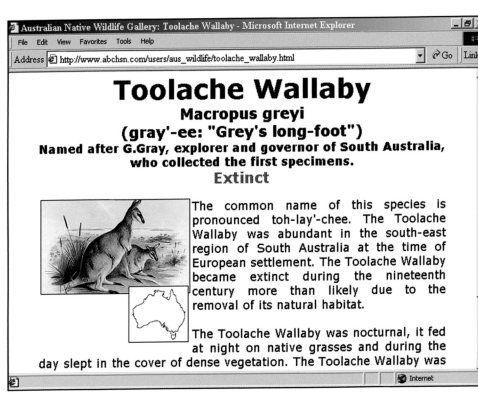

🗗 Australian Native Wildlife Gallery: Toolache Wallaby - Microsoft Internet Explorer   _ | 🗗 | ✕

File   Edit   View   Favorites   Tools   Help

Address 🖹 http://www.abchsn.com/users/aus_wildlife/toolache_wallaby.html   ▾   ⭯ Go   Link

Toolache Wallaby
Macropus greyi
(gray'-ee: "Grey's long-foot")
Named after G.Gray, explorer and governor of South Australia, who collected the first specimens.
Extinct

The common name of this species is pronounced toh-lay'-chee. The Toolache Wallaby was abundant in the south-east region of South Australia at the time of European settlement. The Toolache Wallaby became extinct during the nineteenth century more than likely due to the removal of its natural habitat.

The Toolache Wallaby was nocturnal, it fed at night on native grasses and during the day slept in the cover of dense vegetation. The Toolache Wallaby was

🖹   🌐 Internet

⚠ *The toolache wallaby, extinct since the 1930s, most likely lost its battle for survival once European settlement moved into its habitat in South Australia.*

One day, without warning, a bulldozer cut a path through the wallaby's habitat. The bulldozer was part of a survey team that was searching out a location for a new development. Although the bulldozer was stopped before it harmed any wallabies, the Proserpine rock wallaby and other wallaby species continue to be threatened by habitat loss, hunting, predators, and competition for food from other animals.[1]

It is already too late for one species—the toolache wallaby. In the early twentieth century, the toolache wallaby's habitat had been destroyed to allow farming and sheep grazing. Prized for its fur, the species was also a popular hunting target. By 1923, only fourteen members of this species remained, and efforts to protect these last few animals were unsuccessful. As a result, the toolache wallaby has been considered extinct since 1939.

Habitat Loss

According to the Australian Conservation Foundation, Australia has the highest rate of land clearing of any developed nation. The loss of habitat is a major threat to all of Australia's animals, but it is especially threatening to Australia's marsupials. Australian Aboriginal people, who first arrived on the continent between 40,000 and 60,000 years ago, frequently burned wallaby habitat to flush the animals out so that they could hunt them more easily. In modern times, land has been cleared for agriculture and urban development. This shrinks wallaby habitat or breaks it into fragments. Farm animals compact topsoil as they graze and roam, also destroying wallaby habitat.

In addition, human development has introduced new plant species to Australia. For example, black-footed rock wallabies, mostly found in Australia's Northern Territory,

depend on native grasses, shrubs, and fruits. However, nonnative buffel grass is replacing some of the native plants that the rock wallabies like to eat.

Fire is still a problem as well, although controlled fires benefit many species of plant and animal life. If not controlled, brushfires become wildfires that can destroy large areas of wallaby habitat, particularly the dense lower layers that wallabies use for shelter. Some Australian conservationists believe that the Aboriginal burning practices helped wallaby and kangaroo populations to thrive, even though Aboriginal people hunted them, because controlled fires kept wildfires from erupting.

▷ Hunting for Sport and Profit

Many mammals, including humans, maintain a basic size once they reach adulthood. However, kangaroos and wallabies continue to grow more robust throughout their lives, and the males of these species become more muscular, especially in the shoulders and forearms. Yet, because of hunting, the average size of Australian marsupials has shrunk over time. For centuries, hunters have targeted the largest animals they could find, leaving smaller ones to reproduce.

Aboriginal people have hunted kangaroos and wallabies for thousands of years. The earliest aboriginal hunting method probably involved trapping the animals in a deep pit. Later, various hunting tools included nets, spears, boomerangs, and, most effectively, guns. Aboriginal people ate the meat of kangaroos and wallabies, and they also used their muscle sinew for twine and their teeth for necklaces. Skins might be made into water bags or coats. Residents of New Guinea, for example, still hunt the agile wallaby species, which can weigh up to 50 pounds (22.7 kilograms). One hunting method is to burn grass in the dry season,

▲ Australia's Aboriginal people had an effect upon the continent's native animals, including wallabies. This Aboriginal cave painting of a wallaby is found in Kakadu National Park.

which grows back in a thick, green carpet. When agile wallabies come to feed on the grass, they are ambushed by hunting dogs.

By the late eighteenth century, Europeans began to arrive in Australia. As they built communities and cleared land for farming, these new Australians began to view kangaroos and wallabies as pests. Hunting clubs were formed to kill these animals—both for sport and to help keep them off private property. In modern times, wallabies and

kangaroos are still killed in large numbers for their skins and their meat, which is mostly used for animal food. However, the Australian government has taken steps to make sure that hunters do not kill too many of any one species. Quotas, or limits on the number of animals that can be killed, have been placed on several species, including the whiptail wallaby.

▷ Predators and Feral Animals

Feral animals are one of the most widespread threats to wallaby species. In Australia, feral cats have been found that weigh more than 30 pounds (13.6 kilograms). Feral goats, pigs, and rabbits also compete with wallabies and kangaroos for food. In addition, they eat or trample the vegetation that wallabies rely on for protection from predators. Some estimates place more than 200 million rabbits roaming the Australian continent, which disturbs the native habitat and leads to native animals becoming endangered.

Feral cats and foxes, which were introduced into the country either as pets or for sport, now number in the millions. Feral cats prey on dozens of native species and are especially known

Wallabies and kangaroos are still hunted and killed for their skins and their meat and because they are considered pests by both farmers and ranchers.

▲ *Australian wild dogs called dingoes have been known to prey on wallabies, but they also prey on feral cats and foxes, which kill many wallabies.*

for killing joeys. In fact, the rarely seen tammar wallaby is nearly extinct on the Australian mainland, and feral cats that prey on the wallabies are the primary threat. Many wallaby protection programs try to reduce the local populations of feral animals.

Sometimes, predators of other animals have a positive effect on wallaby populations. Wild dogs called dingoes can prey on kangaroos and wallabies, but they also target feral cats and foxes. "Although dingoes kill large kangaroos," an Australian park official has said, "they also . . . protect the smaller ones that they don't prey upon."[2]

And some wildlife experts believe that wallaby populations are in much better shape in areas where dingoes are present.

Chapter 4

Concern and Conservation

The last few decades have seen an increase in organized government efforts to protect wallabies. In 1993, Australia's federal government passed an Endangered Species Protection Act that listed endangered and vulnerable species. The act, which has been updated since, also required the development of recovery plans for animals that are endangered or at risk. In 1999, the Environment Protection and

△ Australia's national parks provide a safe haven for wallabies, like these in Kakadu National Park.

Biodiversity Conservation Act created greater protections for endangered wallabies and other species.

Without Australia's national parks, Australia's wallabies would have little hope. In addition to protecting ample wallaby habitats, parks can provide safe environments from predators and introduced species. In 2003, the Australian Foundation for National Parks & Wildlife began a campaign to purchase the Green Gully wilderness area, one of the last strongholds for brush-tailed rock wallabies. Other conservation programs include captive breeding to increase wallaby populations, feral animal control, and measures to protect habitat. Sometimes, officials and private citizens change brush-burning and grazing activities to protect sensitive wallaby habitat.

Captive Breeding

Captive breeding combined with feral animal control and habitat protection has proven to be one of the most successful ways to conserve wallaby populations. Captive breeding means that wallabies are allowed to breed in a safe environment, such as a zoo. After a while, the offspring are "reintroduced" into their native habitats throughout Australia. Several parks host captive breeding programs that help to boost wallaby populations, and they have been mostly successful. In 1995, conservation officials established a captive breeding program for bridled nail-tailed wallabies at Idalia National Park in Queensland. The program began with 170 wallabies. By 2002, that number had grown to about 700 individuals.

Often, Australia's islands are special refuges for endangered species. For example, off the coast of Western Australia, islands are home to populations of the banded hare wallaby and other endangered marsupials. Because

they are surrounded by water, islands are less likely to become overrun with feral animals. Sometimes, wallabies are bred in captivity on an island and then brought back to the mainland.

One of the most interesting situations occurred on Kawau, an island in New Zealand's Hauraki Gulf. There, brush-tailed rock wallabies, tammar wallabies, parma wallabies, and swamp wallabies were introduced in the 1830s. The wallabies became so plentiful that they were thought to have eaten all the available food. In 2003, conservationists were working to move some of the tammar and brush-tailed rock wallabies from Kawau into a captive-breeding program on the Australian mainland. The tammar wallabies from Kawau are the only remaining members of that subspecies, which is extinct on the mainland.

"Islands can act as staging posts that, for some species at least, provide us with more time to grapple with the threatening processes on the mainland," says marsupial zoologist Chris Dickman. "They could one day be used to help repopulate the mainland if the threatening processes can be dealt with."[1]

▷ Animal Control

In Australia, feral animal control is the name of the conservation game. Government officials surround marsupial breeding grounds with poisoned bait, which attracts and kills foxes and feral cats. Another form of animal control comes from electric fences. Endangered marsupials thrive in these fenced "earth sanctuaries," while feral predators are kept out. Australian officials also sometimes encourage the development of "feral-free" buffer zones around park areas.

In 2003, the Australian Wildlife Conservancy began construction on a "feral-proof fence" that will surround a

20,000-acre (8,093.7-hectare) section of the Scotia Wildlife Sanctuary in New South Wales. Members of the conservancy say that when all feral animals inside the fence are removed, it will be the largest area on mainland Australia free of feral cats, foxes, rabbits, and goats. The organization plans to establish populations of several endangered mammal species, including the bridled nail-tailed wallaby. Already, the organization owns twelve sanctuaries that protect about 1.5 million acres (607,028 hectares) of habitat for rock wallabies and other native animals.

"Within five years, we hope Scotia will be home to self-sustaining, wild populations of at least seven threatened

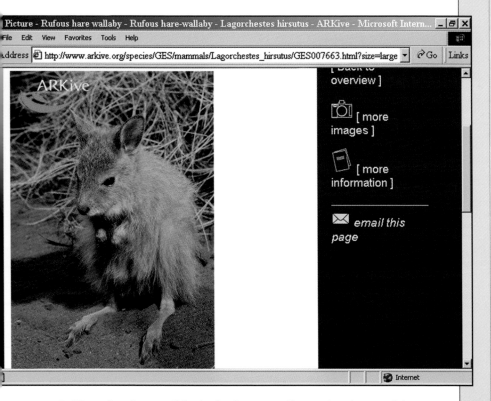

Picture - Rufous hare wallaby - Rufous hare-wallaby - Lagorchestes hirsutus - ARKive - Microsoft Intern...

File   Edit   View   Favorites   Tools   Help

Address http://www.arkive.org/species/GES/mammals/Lagorchestes_hirsutus/GES007663.html?size=large   Go   Links

ARKive

[Back to overview]

[more images]

[more information]

email this page

Internet

▲ The rufous hare wallaby is also known as the western hare wallaby, the mala, and the spinifex rat. The latter name comes from a spiny grass found in the sandy areas of this wallaby's habitat.

mammals . . . ," says Australian Wildlife Conservancy spokesman Atticus Fleming. "To return these mammals to the wild . . . would be an historic moment for conservation in Australia."[2]

In Mutawintji National Park, which is in New South Wales, the population of yellow-footed rock wallabies has steadily increased from an estimated low of thirty-five individuals, thanks to pest-control efforts. These wallabies are often kicked out of their rocky homes by feral goats, which enjoy the same habitat. In 2000, the population of Mutawintji rock wallabies was thriving—estimated to be between three hundred and four hundred animals. The wallabies had recolonized in an area they had not been spotted in for nearly two decades.

Animal control is just part of a larger conservation plan for wallabies. In South Australia, the conservation management plan for the endangered yellow-footed rock wallaby involves the control of both nonnative animals and plants. The aim is not only to protect the wallaby from predators but also to create the best possible habitat by protecting native plants. A recovery plan for brush-tailed rock wallabies includes feral fox baiting and goat reduction. The plan also calls for controls on the local populations of the common eastern gray kangaroo. The kangaroos compete with the rarer wallabies for food and habitat.

▷ Caution: Wallaby Crossing

Sometimes even simple measures go a long way toward protecting endangered wallabies. In Darwin, Australia, wild wallabies living in a city park had become very popular with tourists and residents. Unfortunately, people were often accidentally hitting and killing the animals with their cars. The city responded by installing speed bumps in

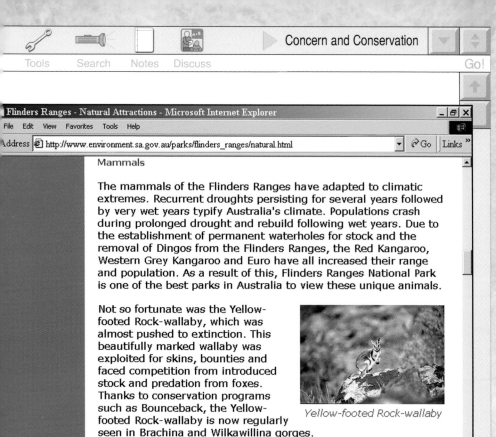

Flinders Ranges - Natural Attractions - Microsoft Internet Explorer

File   Edit   View   Favorites   Tools   Help

Address http://www.environment.sa.gov.au/parks/flinders_ranges/natural.html   Go   Links

Mammals

The mammals of the Flinders Ranges have adapted to climatic extremes. Recurrent droughts persisting for several years followed by very wet years typify Australia's climate. Populations crash during prolonged drought and rebuild following wet years. Due to the establishment of permanent waterholes for stock and the removal of Dingos from the Flinders Ranges, the Red Kangaroo, Western Grey Kangaroo and Euro have all increased their range and population. As a result of this, Flinders Ranges National Park is one of the best parks in Australia to view these unique animals.

Not so fortunate was the Yellow-footed Rock-wallaby, which was almost pushed to extinction. This beautifully marked wallaby was exploited for skins, bounties and faced competition from introduced stock and predation from foxes. Thanks to conservation programs such as Bounceback, the Yellow-footed Rock-wallaby is now regularly seen in Brachina and Wilkawillina gorges.

Yellow-footed Rock-wallaby

Done   Internet

The yellow-footed rock wallaby, nearly extinct, is now regularly seen in the Flinders Ranges National Park in South Australia.

some locations, which cut wallaby deaths by more than 35 percent.

In addition, cars throughout Australia are often outfitted with "roo bars," which protect cars from damage during collisions with kangaroos. But inventors have also developed solutions that protect both cars and wallabies—including devices that make high-frequency sounds to scare away animals. In Queensland, transportation officials and animal researchers have tested the placement of wildlife reflectors in areas visited by Proserpine rock wallabies. Along with speed-reduction signs, the reflectors seem to have been effective.

▲ *Australian Aboriginal people, who arrived on the continent between forty thousand and sixty thousand years ago, hunted wallabies and burned wallaby habitat. But they did not harm wallaby populations nearly as much as European settlers would, later on.*

▷ Bouncing Back

One of Australia's most successful conservation programs is called Operation Bounceback. Begun in Flinders Ranges National Park in 1992, the program takes a larger approach to conservation rather than focusing on a single species such as the yellow-footed rock wallaby. This program includes feral animal control, weed control, replanting of certain native plants, and animal recovery plans. In 1998, an updated version of the program, called Bounceback 2000, was created. Bounceback 2000 expands the original program to include the Gammon Ranges National Park and other areas of the North Flinders Ranges. The goal of the updated program is to promote biological diversity in a much wider region.

Hope for Hoppers: The Future of the Wallaby

At universities, parks, and zoos across Australia, research into the world of wallabies continues. In 2002, the Australian federal government issued a long-range plan for the conservation of kangaroos and wallabies in South Australia. Like Bounceback 2000, the goal of the plan is to take a broader

Macquarie University Public Relations home - Microsoft Internet Explorer

File   Edit   View   Favorites   Tools   Help

Address   http://www.pr.mq.edu.au/events/archive.asp?ItemID=300   Go   Links

High Schools
Sculpture Park
Macquarie Trio
Theatre of Image
Macquarie Singers
Subscribe Here
hsc & beyond
★ postgrad & beyond

Seventy-seven years after it was first identified by a European, an unusual-looking Australian wallaby distinguishable by the beautiful purple pigmentation of the fur around its face and neck, will finally receive its own name and unique status thanks to the latest genetic technology and the hard work of a Macquarie University research team.

The Purple-neck Rock Wallaby [Petrogale Purpureicollis], which inhabits the Mt Isa region in Northwest Queensland, was identified and named by biologist AS Le Souf in 1924. However, authorities refused to believe that the animal existed, and for the next three-quarters of a century the Purple-neck was mistakenly grouped with other rock wallaby species – until now.

Dr Mark Eldridge, of Macquarie University's Department of Biological Sciences, says Le Souf's sighting was disputed because of the rarity of purple among Australian mammals.

"No-one believed him, everyone just said 'No, they can't have purple necks, they must be rubbing themselves on some rock and getting this funny colouration'," Eldridge says. "Because it is secreted through the skin, once the animal is dead the pigment rapidly fades, so by the time Le Souf got the specimens back to Brisbane or Sydney from North Queensland, the colour had gone - so it just looked like a very plain, normal-looking rock wallaby."

Error on page.   Internet

▲ The existence of the purple-neck rock wallaby was debated for years. Researchers at an Australian university have now identified it as a separate species whose unique coloration comes naturally: The purple pigment of its face and neck is secreted through the skin.

approach to the conservation and management of macropod species. At some field stations, kangaroos and wallabies have been fitted with radio collars so that researchers can monitor their behavior. In central Australia, for example, the WWF Australia has worked with land management officials to conduct surveys of the black-footed rock wallaby at ten observation stations. (The WWF used to be known as the World Wildlife Fund and the World Wide Fund for Nature). Reintroduction programs also continue to benefit wallaby populations.

New Discoveries

Australia's unique ecosystem means that scientists are likely to continue making discoveries about wallabies for many years to come. Recently, scientists confirmed a new species known as the purple-neck rock wallaby. Since the species was first spotted in 1924, observers had noted that the animal had distinctive purple or pinkish coloring around its head. However, because the pigment appears and disappears within hours, scientists were not convinced that this wallaby represented a new species. By the time they could examine samples of the purple-neck wallaby, its color had disappeared. At first, scientists thought that the purple-neck wallaby was actually a member of the black-footed rock wallaby species. However, scientists knew that the animals looked different.

"The wallabies weren't accepted by the scientific community as a separate species," says Dr. Mark Eldridge, a Macquarie University biologist who helped to research the new species. "The scientists thought that the [purple color] had come from animals rubbing themselves up against rocks, or perhaps a stain from the vegetation."[1] Finally, in 2001, the purple-neck rock wallaby was recognized as a distinct species.

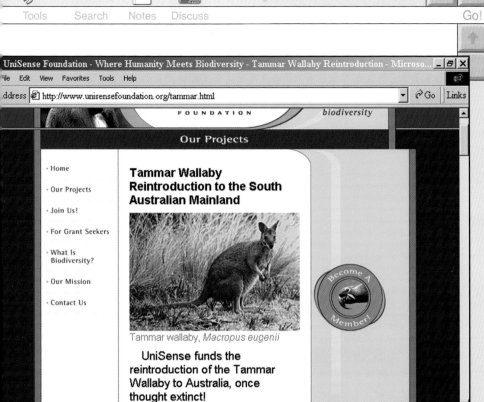

UniSense Foundation - Where Humanity Meets Biodiversity - Tammar Wallaby Reintroduction - Microso...

File   Edit   View   Favorites   Tools   Help

ddress http://www.unisensefoundation.org/tammar.html   Go   Links

FOUNDATION   *biodiversity*

Our Projects

- Home
- Our Projects
- Join Us!
- For Grant Seekers
- What Is Biodiversity?
- Our Mission
- Contact Us

Tammar Wallaby Reintroduction to the South Australian Mainland

Tammar wallaby, *Macropus eugenii*

UniSense funds the reintroduction of the Tammar Wallaby to Australia, once thought extinct!

Internet

◢ *The tammar wallaby is named for the once-common Tamma thickets where it made its home. It is also credited with being the first "kangaroo" to be seen by Europeans when a Dutch ship became stranded off the Australian coast in 1629.*

▷ Testing Tammars

On Kangaroo Island, off the South Australia coast, researchers are studying the tammar wallaby, which has the potential to be repopulated on the mainland. The tammar is nearly extinct on the mainland but is thriving on Kangaroo Island, where it is largely free of predators. Scientists are working to prove that, even without predators, tammar wallabies instinctively get startled at the sight of dangerous mammals. As part of the study, researchers presented the

wallabies with a realistic stuffed fox and cat, which caused the wallabies to stomp their feet or stop eating to look around. The more scared the wallabies get, the more likely they are to run or protect themselves in the wild, the researchers believe.

This research shows that tammar wallabies will have a good chance of survival when they are reintroduced on Australia's mainland. They are already adaptable creatures. In addition to eating grass, tammar wallabies will eat herbs, shrubs, small trees, and some plant seedlings. Tammars also can survive without freshwater supplies and have even been known to drink salty seawater.

Some wallaby research might be considered strange or controversial. In Melbourne, a research institute has tested growing tammar wallaby eggs in mice. This complex process—called xenotransplantation—uses the mice as an

▲ *A young girl feeds an orphaned wallaby joey. Many ordinary Australians have opened their hearts and homes to these young marsupials, although their care is probably best left to wildlife experts.*

incubator for the wallaby eggs. If this method proves to be successful, researchers say that it could one day be used to increase the numbers of animals in species that are considered endangered. During the research, when the eggs grew to maturity, they were transferred to a wallaby to continue their development. "I think we will see animals born from xenotransplantation in the near future," one of the researchers said.[2]

The Power of People

Ordinary citizens are also becoming more and more involved in protecting wallabies. Farmers, who often were responsible for destroying wallaby habitat, now take a more active role in their protection, and some private farmers and ranchers will even declare part of their property a nature preserve. At one such preserve run by a cattle rancher, groups of bridled nail-tailed wallabies have been released and seem to be doing well. Elsewhere, a group called the Friends of the Brush-tailed Rock Wallaby has worked to raise money for research and recovery efforts. In 2003, the Friends group effort helped to fund the release of two male rock wallabies into a group of females. Soon afterward, the colony had young joeys for the first time in five years.

Because so many adult wallabies have been killed, there are many orphaned joeys. Good-hearted Australian citizens sometimes raise the orphaned animals themselves and keep them as pets. Although animals have been saved this way, Australian officials urge citizens to bring orphaned joeys to wildlife rehabilitation centers so that the animals can be released again into the wild.

In the United States, several zoos have wallaby exhibits. The Phoenix Zoo has even created a Wallaby Walkabout, where no fences or barriers separate visitors from a small

This albino Bennett's wallaby is one of the largest wallaby species.

group of Bennett's wallabies. With its black nose and white stripe over its lip, the Bennett's wallaby is tough to miss. It is also one of the largest wallabies, weighing up to 40 pounds (18 kilograms). According to officials with the Phoenix Zoo, Bennett's wallabies might live for fifteen years in the wild, but in captivity they can survive nearly twice as long. This gives researchers more time to study the animal and learn how to help the species survive in the wild. Several other zoos in the United States feature similar walk-through exhibits.

Although many people still consider the kangaroo to be the main symbol of Australia, their smaller cousins—the wallabies—are increasingly cherished for their beauty and rarity, and they are at enormous risk. Like all marsupials, wallabies are living links to Australia's ancient past. Their survival would help to ensure that Australia's wild landscape remains healthy and diverse well into the future.

This series is based on the Endangered and Threatened Wildlife list compiled by the U.S. Fish and Wildlife Service (USFWS). Each book explores an endangered or threatened animal, tells why it has become endangered or threatened, and explains the efforts being made to restore the species' population.

The United States Fish and Wildlife Service, in the Department of the Interior, and the National Marine Fisheries Service, in the Department of Commerce, share responsibility for administration of the Endangered Species Act.

In 1973, Congress took the farsighted step of creating the Endangered Species Act, widely regarded as the world's strongest and most effective wildlife conservation law. It set an ambitious goal: to reverse the alarming trend of human-caused extinction that threatened the ecosystems we all share.

The complete list of Endangered and Threatened Wildlife and Plants can be found at **http://endangered.fws.gov/wildlife.html#Species**.

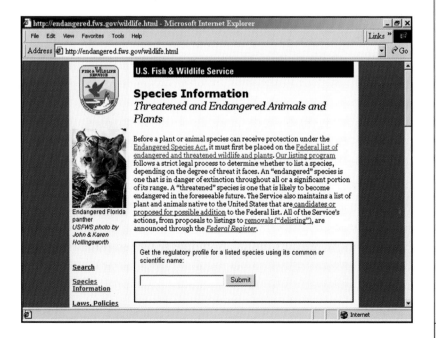

Chapter 1. Lost and Found: Rediscovering Wallabies
1. Michael Szabo, "Australia's Marsupials," *New Scientist,* January 28, 1995, p. 3,030.

Chapter 2. The Real "Big Foot"
1. Terry Domico, *Kangaroos: The Marvelous Mob* (New York: Facts on File, 1993), p. 8.

Chapter 3. Hunting, Habitat Loss, and Other Threats
1. Greg Roberts, "Bulldozer Rips into Rare Wallaby Habitat," *Sydney Morning Herald,* October 15, 1997, p. 10.

2. Terry Domico, *Kangaroos: The Marvelous Mob* (New York: Facts on File, 1993), p. 65.

Chapter 4. Concern and Conservation
1. Michael Szabo, "Australia's Marsupials," *New Scientist,* January 28, 1995, p. 3,030.

2. Australian Wildlife Conservancy press release, "Australia's Largest Feral-free Sanctuary to Save Endangered Mammals," November 29, 2003, <http://www.australianwildlife.org/ Scotia_Media_Release.pdf> (May 5, 2004).

Chapter 5. Hope for Hoppers: The Future of the Wallaby
1. Danny Kingsley, "Purple Wallaby a True-Blue Species," *ABC Science Online,* October 23, 2001, <www.abc .net.au/science/news/stories/s397200.htm> (May 5, 2004).

2. Heather Catchpole, "Wallaby Eggs Grown in Mice," *ABC Science Online,* January 20, 2004, <www.abc.net.au/ science/news/enviro/EnviroRepublish_1027942.htm> (May 5, 2004).

Further Reading

Alter, Judy. *Discovering Australia's Land, People, and Wildlife.* Berkeley Heights, N.J.: Enslow Publishers, Inc., 2004.

Arnold, Caroline. *Australian Animals.* New York: HarperCollins, 2000.

Bartlett, Anne. *The Aboriginal Peoples of Australia.* Minneapolis: Lerner Publications, 2002.

Fenton, Julie A. *Kangaroos and Other Marsupials.* Chicago: World Book, 2000.

Johnston, Marianne. *Wallabies and Their Babies.* New York: PowerKids Press, 1999.

Kavanagh, James. *Australian Wildlife.* Chandler, Ariz.: Waterford Press, Ltd., 1999.

Landau, Elaine. *Australia and New Zealand.* New York: Children's Press, 1999.

Parish, Steve. *Australian Rare and Endangered Wildlife.* Broomall, Pa.: Mason Crest Publishers, 2003.

Porter, Malcolm, and Keith Lye. *Australia and the Pacific.* Austin: Raintree Steck-Vaughn, 2001.

Slater, Pat. *Australian Kangaroos and Wallabies.* Broomall, Pa.: Mason Crest Publishers, 2003.

Swan, Erin Pembrey. *Kangaroos and Koalas: What They Have in Common.* New York: Franklin Watts, 2000.

———.*Uluru, Australia's Aboriginal Heart.* New York: Clarion Books, 2003.

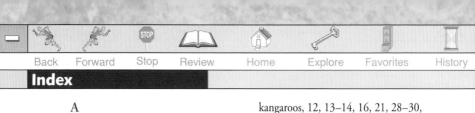
Index